Diabetes Cookbook: save time and money

The Right Book for You

Evelin Turk

Table of Contents

Grilled Chicken And Clementine Kebabs

Servings: 4

Ingredients:

1-pound boneless skinless chicken breasts, cut into 1-inch pieces

2 clementines, unpeeled, each cut into 8 wedges

1 large red onion, cut into 1-inch pieces

1 red bell pepper, cut into 1-inch pieces

2 tablespoons chopped fresh mint

2 1/2 teaspoons extra virgin olive oil

1 teaspoon ground coriander

1/2 teaspoon kosher salt

1/4 teaspoon freshly ground pepper

Directions:

1. Prepare the grill or heat a large grill pan over medium-high heat.

2. Combine the chicken, clementines, onion, bell pepper, mint, 2 teaspoons of the oil, the coriander, salt, and ground pepper in a large bowl and toss to coat. Thread the chicken, clementines, onion, and bell pepper onto eight 8- to 10-inch metal skewers.

3. Brush the grill rack or grill pan with the remaining 1⁄2 teaspoon oil. Place the kebabs on the grill rack or in the grill pan and grill, turning often, until the juices of the chicken run clear, 8 to 10 minutes. Divide the kebabs among 4 plates and serve at once.

Nutrition Info:

9 g carb, 185 cal, 6 g fat, 1 g sat fat, 63 mg chol, 2 g fib, 24 g pro, 197 mg sod • Carb Choices: 1⁄2; Exchanges: 1⁄2 fruit, 1 veg, 3 lean protein, 1⁄2 fat

Edamame Guacamole

Servings: 2 Cups

Ingredients:

1 3/4 cups frozen shelled edamame, thawed

1/2 avocado, pitted, peeled, and chopped

1 small scallion, chopped

1 small jalapeño, seeded and chopped

1 garlic clove, minced

1/2 teaspoon ground cumin

3 tablespoons lime juice

1/4 cup fresh cilantro leaves

3/4 cup cold water

1/2 teaspoon kosher salt

1 plum tomato, diced

Directions:

1. Bring a medium saucepan of water to a boil over high heat. Add the edamame and cook until tender, about 5 minutes. Drain in a colander and rinse with cold running water until cool.

2. Combine the edamame and the remaining ingredients except the tomato in a food processor and process until smooth. Serve at once, or refrigerate, covered, for up to 3 days. To serve, spoon the guacamole into a shallow serving bowl and sprinkle with the tomato.

Nutrition Info:

6 g carb, 69 cal, 3 g fat, 0 g sat fat, 0 mg chol, 3 g fib, 4 g pro, 86 mg sod • Carb Choices: 1/2; Exchanges: 1/2 starch, 1 plant-based protein, 1/2 fat

Ceviche-style Shrimp Salad

Servings: 4

Ingredients:

1/4 cup orange juice

2 tablespoons lime juice

1 1/2 tablespoons extra virgin olive oil

1/2 teaspoon kosher salt

12 ounces large cooked peeled deveined shrimp

1 hothouse (English) cucumber, halved lengthwise and sliced

1 red bell pepper, cut into short, thin strips

1/4 cup chopped fresh cilantro

2 tablespoons diced red onion

1 tablespoon minced jalapeño, including seeds (or to taste)

Directions:

1. Whisk together the orange juice, lime juice, oil, and salt in a large bowl. Add the shrimp, cucumber, bell pepper, cilantro, onion, and jalapeño and toss to coat. Refrigerate the salad, covered, until chilled, at least 2 hours and up to 4 hours.

Nutrition Info:

8 g carb, 162 cal, 6 g fat, 1 g sat fat, 166 mg chol, 1 g fib, 19 g pro, 334 mg sod • Carb Choices: 1/2; Exchanges: 1/2 carb, 3 lean protein, 1 fat

Basil Pesto

Servings: 1/2 Cup

Ingredients:

1⁄4 cup pine nuts, toasted

1 cup tightly packed fresh basil leaves

1 ounce freshly grated Parmesan (about 1⁄4 cup)

3 tablespoons extra-virgin olive oil

1 tablespoon lemon juice

1 small garlic clove, chopped

1⁄4 teaspoon kosher salt

Directions:

1. Combine all the ingredients in a food processor and process until the mixture is finely chopped. The sauce can be refrigerated, with the surface covered with plastic wrap, for up to 4 days.

Nutrition Info:

1 g carb, 89 cal, 9 g fat, 1 g sat fat, 2 mg chol, 0 g fib, 2 g pro, 74 mg sod • Carb Choices: 0; Exchanges: 2 fat

Fish Fillets with Tomato, Bell Pepper, And Basil

Servings: 4

Ingredients:

2 teaspoons extra virgin olive oil

1 medium onion, halved lengthwise and thinly sliced

1 small yellow bell pepper, thinly sliced

1 small red bell pepper, thinly sliced

2 garlic cloves, minced

1/2 cup dry white wine

1 large tomato, chopped

2 tablespoons chopped fresh basil

1/2 teaspoon kosher salt, divided

1/4 teaspoon freshly ground pepper, divided

4 (5-ounce) thick white-fleshed fish fillets

2 tablespoons chopped fresh basil

Directions:

1. Heat a large nonstick skillet over high heat. Add the oil and tilt the pan to coat the bottom evenly. Add the onion and bell peppers to the skillet and cook, stirring often, until the vegetables are softened, 5 minutes. Stir in the garlic and cook, stirring constantly, until fragrant, 30 seconds.

2. Add the wine and bring to a boil, stirring to scrape up the browned bits from the bottom of the skillet. Cook until almost all the liquid is evaporated, about 5 minutes. Add the tomato, basil, 1/4 teaspoon of the salt, and 1/8 teaspoon of the ground pepper and return to a boil.

3. Sprinkle the fish with the remaining 1/4 teaspoon salt and remaining 1/8 teaspoon ground pepper. Arrange the fillets in a single layer on top of the vegetables. Cover, reduce the heat, and simmer until the fish flakes easily with a fork, 6 to 8 minutes. Divide the fish evenly among 4 plates. Stir the basil into the vegetables and spoon evenly over the fish. Serve at once.

Nutrition Info:

9 g carb, 185 cal, 3 g fat, 1 g sat fat, 54 mg chol, 2 g fib, 24 g pro, 222 mg sod •
Carb Choices: 1/2; Exchanges: 1 veg, 3 lean protein, 1/2 fat

Osso Buco–style Turkey Drumsticks

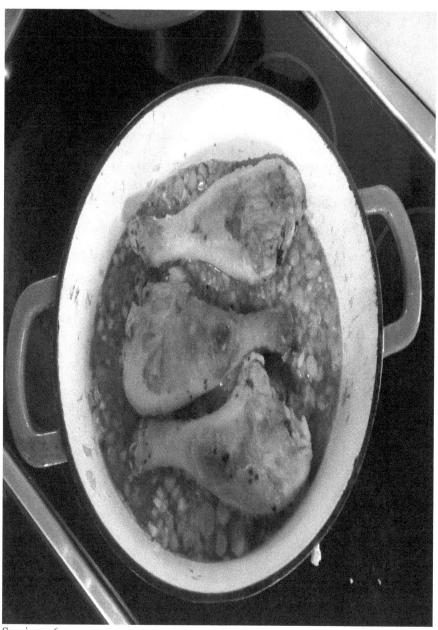

Servings: 6

Ingredients:

6 (10- to 12-ounce) turkey drumsticks, skinned

1/2 teaspoon kosher salt

1/2 teaspoon freshly ground pepper

4 teaspoons extra virgin olive oil, divided

2 carrots, peeled and chopped

2 stalks celery, chopped

1 medium onion, chopped

2 garlic cloves, minced

3/4 cup dry white wine

13/4 cups Chicken Stock or low-sodium chicken broth

1 (141/2-ounce) can no-salt-added diced tomatoes

3 tablespoons no-salt-added tomato paste

1 bay leaf

Directions:

1. Preheat the oven to 325°F.

2. Sprinkle the drumsticks with the salt and pepper. Heat a large skillet over medium-high heat. Add 2 teaspoons of the oil and tilt the pan to coat the bottom evenly. Add the drumsticks and cook, turning often, until well browned on all sides, about 10 minutes. Transfer to a large roasting pan.

3. Add the remaining 2 teaspoons oil and tilt the pan to coat the bottom evenly. Add the carrots, celery, and onion to the skillet and cook, stirring often, until the vegetables soften and begin to brown, 8 minutes. Add the garlic and cook, stirring constantly, until fragrant, 30 seconds. Add the wine and bring to a boil, stirring to scrape up the browned bits from the bottom of the skillet. Cook until most of the liquid evaporates, 2 minutes. Stir in the stock, tomatoes, tomato paste, and bay leaf and bring to a boil. Carefully pour the mixture over the turkey. Cover tightly with foil and bake until the turkey is very tender, about 2 hours. Remove and discard the bay leaf.

4. Transfer the turkey to 6 deep bowls and spoon the sauce and vegetables evenly over the turkey.

Nutrition Info:

9 g carb, 318 cal, 9 g fat, 2 g sat fat, 168 mg chol, 2 g fib, 43 g pro, 269 mg sod • Carb Choices: 1/2; Exchanges: 1 veg, 6 lean protein, 1/2 fat

Baked Scallops Au Gratin

Servings: 4

Ingredients:

1/2 teaspoon canola oil

1-pound sea scallops

2/3 cup panko crumbs

2 tablespoons unsalted butter, melted

2 tablespoons lemon juice

1 garlic clove, minced

1/2 teaspoon kosher salt

1/4 teaspoon freshly ground pepper

Directions:

1. Preheat the oven to 425°F. Brush a 13 x 9-inch baking dish with the oil.

2. Pat the scallops dry and place in the prepared baking dish.

3. Combine the panko crumbs, butter, lemon juice, garlic, salt, and pepper in a small bowl and stir until the crumbs are moistened. Sprinkle the crumb mixture over the scallops.

4. Bake until the scallops are opaque in the center and the crumbs are lightly browned, 15 to 18 minutes. Divide the scallops evenly among 4 plates, top evenly with any crumbs remaining in the dish, and serve at once.

Nutrition Info:

11 g carb, 194 cal, 7 g fat, 4 g sat fat, 52 mg chol, 0 g fib, 21 g pro, 346 mg sod • Carb Choices: 1/2; Exchanges: 1/2 starch, 3 lean protein, 1 fat

Lemon Chicken And Snow Pea Stir-fry

Servings: 4

Ingredients:

1/2 cup Chicken Stock or low-sodium chicken broth

2 tablespoons reduced-sodium soy sauce

2 teaspoons grated lemon zest

2 tablespoons lemon juice

2 teaspoons cornstarch

1 teaspoon sugar

4 teaspoons canola oil, divided

1-pound boneless skinless chicken breast, cut into thin strips

2 garlic cloves, minced

4 cups snow peas, trimmed and cut in half on the diagonal

2 scallions, thinly sliced

Directions:

1. Combine the stock, soy sauce, lemon zest, lemon juice, cornstarch, and sugar in a small bowl and stir until the cornstarch and sugar dissolve.

2. Heat a large wok or nonstick skillet over medium-high heat. Add 2 teaspoons of the oil and tilt the pan to coat the bottom evenly. Add the chicken and cook, stirring constantly, until lightly browned, 2 to 3 minutes. Transfer the chicken to a plate and wipe out the wok with paper towels.

3. Add the remaining 2 teaspoons oil to the wok over medium-high heat. Add the garlic and cook, stirring constantly, until fragrant, 30 seconds. Add the snow peas and cook, stirring constantly, until crisp-tender, 3 minutes. Stir in the chicken and the stock mixture and cook until the sauce is thickened, 30 seconds. Remove from the heat and stir in the scallions. Divide evenly among 4 plates and serve at once.

Nutrition Info:

8 g carb, 207 cal, 7 g fat, 1 g sat fat, 63 mg chol, 1 g fib, 25 g pro, 381 mg sod • Carb Choices: 1/2; Exchanges: 1 veg, 3 lean protein, 1 fat

Mushroom And Bulgur–stuffed Cabbage

Servings: 4

Ingredients:

1 large head savoy cabbage

4 teaspoons extra virgin olive oil, divided

1 small onion, chopped

8 ounces cremini or white mushrooms, chopped

1 garlic clove, minced

3⁄4 teaspoon ground cinnamon

1 1⁄2 cups Vegetable Stock or low-sodium vegetable broth

1⁄3 cup medium- or coarse-grind bulgur

1⁄4 cup golden raisins

1⁄2 teaspoon kosher salt

1⁄8 teaspoon freshly ground pepper

1⁄4 cup pine nuts, toasted

2 tablespoons lemon juice

1 (15-ounce) can no-salt-added crushed tomatoes

1 tablespoon white wine vinegar

1 tablespoon honey

Directions:

1. Remove 8 large outer leaves from the cabbage and set aside. From the remaining cabbage, chop 4 cups of cabbage. Reserve the remaining cabbage for another use.

2. Bring a large pot of water to a boil over high heat. Add the large outer cabbage leaves and cook until soft and pliable, about 3 minutes. Drain the cabbage leaves in a colander and rinse under cold running water until cool. Dry the cabbage leaves with paper towels.

3. Heat a large nonstick skillet over medium-high heat. Add 2 teaspoons of the oil and the onion, mushrooms, and chopped cabbage and cook, stirring often, until most of the liquid has evaporated, 8 minutes. Add the garlic and cinnamon and cook, stirring constantly, 30 seconds. Stir in the stock, bulgur, raisins, salt, and pepper and bring to a boil. Cover, reduce the heat, and simmer until the bulgur is tender, 15 minutes. Stir in the pine nuts and lemon juice.

4. Preheat the oven to 350°F. Brush a large casserole dish with the remaining 2 teaspoons oil.

5. Place 1/2 cup of the bulgur mixture in the center of each cabbage leaf. Fold in the sides of the leaf and roll up. Place the rolls, seam side down, in the prepared dish.

6. Stir together the tomatoes, vinegar, and honey in a bowl. Pour the tomato mixture over the cabbage rolls. Cover and bake 45 minutes.

7. Divide the cabbage rolls and sauce evenly among 4 plates.

Nutrition Info:

40 g carb, 285 cal, 11 g fat, 1 g sat fat, 0 mg chol, 8 g fib, 8 g pro, 361 mg sod • Carb Choices: 2 1/2; Exchanges: 1/2 starch, 1 carb, 3 veg, 2 fat

Tuna with Chili-garlic Roasted Onions

Servings: 4

Ingredients:

4 teaspoons canola oil, divided

1 tablespoon lime juice

2 teaspoons chili-garlic paste, divided

1 (1 1/4-pound) tuna steak, about 1-inch thick

2 large sweet onions, halved lengthwise and thinly sliced

1/2 teaspoon kosher salt, divided

1 tablespoon light brown sugar

Directions:

1. Preheat the oven to 400°F.

2. Stir together 1 teaspoon of the oil, the lime juice, and 1 teaspoon of the chili-garlic paste in a shallow dish. Add the tuna and turn to coat. Cover and refrigerate 30 minutes.

3. Meanwhile, place the onions on a large rimmed baking sheet. Drizzle with 2 teaspoons of the remaining oil and sprinkle with 1/4 teaspoon of the salt. Toss to coat. Arrange the onions in a single layer. Bake, stirring once, until tender and lightly browned, about 30 minutes. Maintain the oven

1. temperature.

4. Transfer the onions to a small bowl. Add the sugar and remaining 1 teaspoon chili-garlic paste and stir to combine.

5. Remove the tuna from the marinade and discard the marinade. Sprinkle the tuna with the remaining 1/4 teaspoon salt. Heat a medium ovenproof skillet over medium-high heat. Add the remaining 1 teaspoon oil and tilt the pan to coat the bottom evenly. Place the tuna in the skillet and cook, turning once, 1 minute on each side, or until well browned. Transfer the skillet to the oven and bake 3 minutes for medium rare, or to the desired degree of doneness.

6. Transfer the tuna to a cutting board and cut into thin slices. Divide the tuna and onions evenly among 4 plates and serve at once.

Nutrition Info:

16 g carb, 257 cal, 6 g fat, 1 g sat fat, 62 mg chol, 2 g fib, 33 g pro, 218 mg sod •
Carb Choices: 1; Exchanges: 2 veg, 4 lean protein, 1 fat

Baked Salmon with Cucumber-grape Tomato Salsa

Servings: 4

Ingredients:

2 1/2 teaspoons extra virgin olive oil, divided

4 (4-ounce) salmon fillets

1/2 teaspoon kosher salt, divided

1/8 teaspoon freshly ground pepper

1/2 hothouse (English) cucumber, peeled and chopped

1 1/2 cups grape tomatoes, halved

1 jalapeño, seeded and minced

2 tablespoons minced red onion

2 tablespoons lime juice

2 tablespoons chopped fresh cilantro, basil, mint, or Italian parsley

Directions:

1. Preheat the oven to 400°F. Brush a medium baking dish with 1/2 teaspoon of the oil.

2. Sprinkle the salmon with 1/4 teaspoon of the salt and the pepper. Place in the prepared baking dish and bake until the fish is opaque in the center, 10 to 12 minutes.

3. Meanwhile, combine the cucumber, tomatoes, jalapeño, onion, lime juice, cilantro, remaining 2 teaspoons oil, and remaining 1/4 teaspoon salt in a medium bowl and stir to mix well. Divide the salmon and salsa evenly among 4 plates and serve at once.

Nutrition Info:

4 g carb, 229 cal, 11 g fat, 2 g sat fat, 72 mg chol, 1 g fib, 27 g pro, 200 mg sod • Carb Choices: 0; Exchanges: 4 lean protein, 1/2 fat

Rice with Apple, Pecans, And Rosemary

Servings: 4

Ingredients:

2 teaspoons extra virgin olive oil

1 small apple, peeled, cored, and chopped

1/4 cup diced onion

1/4 cup Vegetable Stock or low-sodium vegetable broth

2 teaspoons chopped fresh rosemary or 1/2 teaspoon crumbled dried rosemary

2 cups cooked brown rice

1/2 teaspoon kosher salt

Pinch of freshly ground pepper

2 tablespoons pecans, toasted and chopped

Directions:

1. Heat a medium nonstick skillet over medium heat. Add the oil and tilt the pan to coat the bottom evenly. Add the apple and onion and cook, stirring often, until softened, 5 minutes.

2. Add the stock and rosemary and bring to a boil over high heat. Reduce the heat and simmer, uncovered, until the apple is tender and most of the liquid has evaporated, about 3 minutes. Add the rice, salt, and pepper and cook, stirring often, until heated through, 2 minutes. Stir in the pecans. Spoon the rice into a serving dish and serve at once.

Nutrition Info:

28 g carb, 173 cal, 6 g fat, 1 g sat fat, 0 mg chol, 3 g fib, 3 g pro, 150 mg sod • Carb Choices: 2; Exchanges: 1 1/2 starch, 1/2 fruit, 1 fat

Wine And Garlic Marinated Grilled Whole Chicken

Servings: 6

Ingredients:

1/4 cup dry white wine

2 teaspoons grated lemon zest

2 tablespoons lemon juice

2 1/2 teaspoons extra virgin olive oil, divided

4 garlic cloves, minced

1 scallion, thinly sliced

1 whole chicken (about 3 1/4 pounds)

1/2 teaspoon kosher salt

1/4 teaspoon freshly ground pepper

Directions:

1. Combine the wine, lemon zest, lemon juice, 2 teaspoons of the oil, the garlic, and scallion in a large shallow glass dish.

2. Remove and discard the neck and giblets from the cavity of the chicken. Place the chicken breast side down on a cutting board. Cut along both sides of the backbone using poultry shears or a sharp knife. Discard the backbone. Press the chicken flat using your palms.

3. Place the chicken in the dish and turn to coat with the marinade. Cover and refrigerate 8 to 12 hours, turning the chicken occasionally.

4. Preheat the grill to medium heat.

5. Remove the chicken from the marinade and discard the marinade. Pat the chicken dry with paper towels. Loosen the skin from the breast and drumsticks by inserting your fingers and gently separating the skin from the meat. Rub the salt and pepper over the breast and drumsticks underneath the skin.

6. Brush the grill rack with the remaining 1/2 teaspoon oil. Place the chicken on the grill skin side down. Cover and grill, turning once, until an instant- read thermometer inserted into a thigh reads 165°F, 50 to 60 minutes.

7. Carve the chicken and divide evenly among 6 plates. Remove the skin before eating.

Nutrition Info:

0 g carb, 155 cal, 5 g fat, 1 g sat fat, 81 mg chol, 0 g fib, 26 g pro, 187 mg sod • Carb Choices: 0; Exchanges: 4 lean protein

Shrimp Pot Stickers with Sweet Soy Dipping Sauce

Servings: 6

Ingredients:

1 cup Chicken Stock or low-sodium chicken broth

4 teaspoons reduced-sodium soy sauce, divided

8 ounces medium cooked peeled deveined shrimp, finely chopped

2 tablespoons minced scallion

2 tablespoons chopped fresh cilantro

2 teaspoons grated fresh ginger

1 large egg white

1 garlic clove, crushed through a press

1/2 teaspoon Asian sesame oil

18 wonton wrappers

4 teaspoons canola oil, divided Sauce

2 tablespoons reduced-sodium soy sauce

1 tablespoon cold water

4 teaspoons mirin

4 teaspoons rice vinegar

1/4 teaspoon Asian sesame oil

1 tablespoon thinly sliced scallion, green tops only

Directions:

1. To make the pot stickers, combine the stock and 2 teaspoons of the soy sauce in a measuring cup. Set aside.

2. Stir together the shrimp, scallion, cilantro, ginger, egg white, garlic, sesame oil, and the remaining 2 teaspoons soy sauce in a medium bowl. Working with 1 wonton wrapper at a time (keep the remaining wrappers covered to prevent drying), place the wonton wrapper on a work surface. Place 1 rounded teaspoon of the shrimp mixture in the center. Moisten the edge of the wrapper with water, bring the opposite corners together, and pinch the edges together to seal. Place the shaped pot stickers on a plate and cover with damp paper towels to prevent drying. Repeat with the remaining wrappers and filling.

3. Heat a large nonstick skillet over medium-high heat. Add 2 teaspoons of the canola oil and tilt the pan to coat the bottom evenly. Add half of the pot stickers and cook until the bottoms are browned, 2 to 3 minutes. Add half of the stock mixture and bring to a boil. Cover and cook until the stock is absorbed, about 3 minutes. Transfer the pot stickers to a large plate and cover to keep warm. Repeat with the remaining 2 teaspoons canola oil, the remaining pot stickers, and the remaining broth mixture. Serve at once with the sauce.

4. To make the sauce, whisk together the soy sauce, water, mirin, vinegar, and oil in a small bowl. Stir in the scallions.

Nutrition Info:

16 g carb, 170 cal, 5 g fat, 0 g sat fat, 79 mg chol, 1 g fib, 14 g pro, 619 mg sod • Carb Choices: 1; Exchanges: 1 starch, 1 lean protein, 1/2 fat

Roasted Pork Tenderloin with Pears And Sage

Servings: 4

Ingredients:

3 teaspoons extra virgin olive oil, divided

1 (1-pound) pork tenderloin, trimmed of all visible fat

4 teaspoons chopped fresh sage or 2 teaspoons crumbled dried sage

1/2 teaspoon plus a pinch of kosher salt, divided

1/4 teaspoon plus 1/8 teaspoon freshly ground pepper, divided

2 ripe pears, cored and sliced

Directions:

1. Preheat the oven to 400°F. Brush a large rimmed baking sheet with 1 teaspoon of the oil.

2. Sprinkle the tenderloin with 2 teaspoons of the sage, 1/2 teaspoon of the salt, and 1/4 teaspoon of the pepper. Place the pork on the prepared baking sheet.

3. Combine the pears, the remaining 2 teaspoons oil, 2 teaspoons sage, 1/8 teaspoon pepper, and pinch of salt in a large bowl and toss to coat. Arrange the pears in a single layer around the pork.

4. Bake, turning the pork and the pears once, until an instant-read thermometer inserted into the center of the tenderloin reads 140°F, 15 to 20 minutes. Cover loosely with foil and let stand about 10 minutes. Cut the tenderloin into thin slices, divide the pork and pears evenly among 4 plates, and serve at once.

Nutrition Info:

13 g carb, 211 cal, 7 g fat, 2 g sat fat, 63 mg chol, 3 g fib, 23 g pro, 203 mg sod •
Carb Choices: 1; Exchanges: 1 fruit, 3 lean protein, 1/2 fat

Pasta And Pea Salad

Servings: 6

Ingredients:

6 ounces whole wheat rotini or other short pasta (about 2 cups)

6 ounces fresh sugar snap peas, trimmed (about 2 cups)

1 cup shelled fresh English peas or unthawed frozen green peas

3 tablespoons white wine vinegar

1 tablespoon extra virgin olive oil

3⁄4 teaspoon kosher salt

1⁄8 teaspoon freshly ground pepper

2 tablespoons finely crumbled feta cheese

2 tablespoons chopped fresh dill

Directions:

1. Bring a large pot of water to a boil over high heat; add the pasta, return to a boil and cook 8 minutes. Add the snap peas and English peas and cook 1 minute. Drain in a colander and rinse under cold running water until cool. Drain well.

2. Meanwhile, whisk together the vinegar, oil, salt, and pepper in a large bowl. Add the pasta mixture, feta, and dill and toss to coat. Serve the salad at room temperature. The salad tastes best on the day it is made, but it can be refrigerated, covered, for up to 2 days. Let stand at room temperature 30 minutes before serving.

Nutrition Info:

23 g carb, 158 cal, 4 g fat, 1 g sat fat, 3 mg chol, 5 g fib, 7 g pro, 181 mg sod • Carb Choices: 11/2; Exchanges: 11/2 starch, 1/2 fat

Asparagus with Sautéed Shiitake Mushrooms

Servings: 4

Ingredients:

1-pound asparagus, tough ends removed

2 teaspoons extra virgin olive oil

6 ounces shiitake mushrooms, stemmed and thinly sliced

1 small shallot, finely chopped

1/4 teaspoon kosher salt

2 teaspoons chopped fresh Italian parsley

Directions:

1. In a saucepan fitted with a steamer basket, bring 1 inch of water to a boil over medium-high heat. Add the asparagus, reduce the heat to low, cover, and steam until tender, 4 to 5 minutes.

2. Meanwhile, heat a medium nonstick skillet over medium-high heat. Add the oil and tilt the pan to coat the bottom evenly. Add the mushrooms, shallots, and salt. Cook, stirring often, until the mushrooms are barely tender, 3 minutes. Remove from the heat and stir in the parsley.

3. To serve, arrange the asparagus on a serving platter and spoon the mushrooms over them. Serve hot, warm, or at room temperature.

Nutrition Info:

7 g carb, 56 cal, 3 g fat, 0 g sat fat, 0 mg chol, 2 g fib, 2 g pro, 73 mg sod • Carb Choices: 1/2; Exchanges: 1 veg, 1/2 fat

Asian Pesto

Servings: 1/2 Cup

Ingredients:

1/4 cup slivered almonds, toasted

1/2 cup tightly packed fresh cilantro leaves

1/2 cup tightly packed fresh basil leaves

1 ounce freshly grated Parmesan (about 1/4 cup)

2 tablespoons cold water

1 tablespoon extra-virgin olive oil

1 tablespoon lime juice

1 tablespoon reduced-sodium soy sauce

1 small garlic clove, chopped

1/4 teaspoon Asian sesame oil

1/4 teaspoon kosher salt

Directions:

1. Combine all the ingredients in a food processor and pulse until the mixture is finely chopped. The sauce can be refrigerated, with the surface covered with plastic wrap, for up to 4 days.

Nutrition Info:

1 g carb, 51 cal, 4 g fat, 1 g sat fat, 2 mg chol, 1 g fib, 2 g pro, 150 mg sod • Carb Choices: 0; Exchanges: 1 fat

Lemon Curd

Servings: 2 1/2 Cups

Ingredients:

1 1/2 cups water

1/2 cup lemon juice

2 large egg yolks

1 cup sugar

1/4 cup cornstarch

Pinch of salt

1 tablespoon unsalted butter

1 tablespoon grated lemon zest

Directions:

1. Combine the water, lemon juice, egg yolks, sugar, cornstarch, and salt in a large saucepan and whisk until smooth. Cook over medium heat, whisking constantly, until the mixture comes to a boil and thickens, about 6 minutes.

2. Remove from the heat and stir in the butter and lemon zest. Spoon into a medium bowl and cover the surface of the curd with wax paper to prevent a skin from forming. Cool to room temperature. Refrigerate until chilled, at least 2 hours and up to a week.

Nutrition Info:

24 g carb, 114 cal, 2 g fat, 1 g sat fat, 44 mg chol, 0 g fib, 1 g pro, 17 mg sod • Carb Choices: 1 1/2; Exchanges: 1 1/2 carb, 1/2 fat

Pork Chops with Apricot-walnut Sauce

Servings: 4

Ingredients:

4 (5-ounce) bone-in center-cut pork loin chops, trimmed of all visible fat

1/2 teaspoon kosher salt

1/8 teaspoon freshly ground pepper

4 teaspoons extra virgin olive oil, divided

2 tablespoons diced onion

1 garlic clove, minced

1/2 cup Chicken Stock or low-sodium chicken broth

1/3 cup chopped dried apricots

1/4 cup orange juice

2 tablespoons walnuts, toasted and chopped

2 teaspoons chopped fresh thyme or 1/2 teaspoon dried thyme

Directions:

1. Sprinkle the chops with the salt and pepper. Heat a large nonstick skillet over medium heat. Add 2 teaspoons of the oil and tilt the pan to coat the bottom evenly. Add the chops and cook, turning once, until well browned and slightly pink in the center, about 3 minutes on each side. Transfer to a plate and cover loosely with foil to keep warm.

2. Add the remaining 2 teaspoons oil to the skillet and tilt to coat the pan. Add the onion and cook, stirring often, until softened, 3 minutes. Add the garlic and cook, stirring constantly, until fragrant, 30 seconds. Add the stock, apricots, and orange juice and bring to a boil, stirring to scrape up the browned bits from the bottom of the pan. Cook until reduced by half. Stir in the walnuts and thyme. Place the chops on 4 plates and spoon the sauce evenly over the chops.

Nutrition Info:

9 g carb, 236 cal, 12 g fat, 3 g sat fat, 59 mg chol, 1 g fib, 22 g pro, 220 mg sod • Carb Choices: 1/2; Exchanges: 1/2 fruit, 3 lean protein, 1 1/2 fat

Pan-seared Scallops with Pineapple-mango Salsa

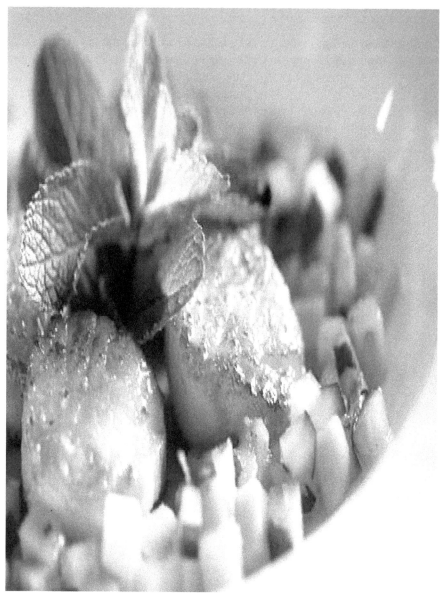

Servings: 4

Ingredients:

1 cup diced pineapple

1 medium mango, peeled, pitted, and diced

2 tablespoons minced red onion

1 tablespoon lime juice

1 tablespoon chopped fresh mint

4 teaspoons canola oil, divided

1/8 teaspoon plus 1/4 teaspoon ground cumin, divided

1/8 teaspoon plus 1/4 teaspoon ground coriander, divided Pinch plus

1/2 teaspoon kosher salt

1-pound sea scallops

Lime wedges

Directions:

1. Combine the pineapple, mango, onion, lime juice, mint, 2 teaspoons of the oil, 1/8 teaspoon of the cumin, 1/8 teaspoon of the coriander, and the pinch of salt in a large bowl and stir to mix well.

2. Pat the scallops dry and sprinkle with the remaining 1/2 teaspoon salt, remaining 1/4 teaspoon cumin, and remaining 1/4 teaspoon coriander. Heat a large skillet over medium-high heat. Add the remaining 2 teaspoons oil and tilt the pan to coat the bottom evenly. Add the scallops and cook, turning once, until just opaque in the centers, about 1 1/2 minutes on each side. Divide the scallops and salsa among 4 plates and serve at once with the lime wedges.

Nutrition Info:

17 g carb, 196 cal, 6 g fat, 0 g sat fat, 37 mg chol, 1 g fib, 20 g pro, 342 mg sod • Carb Choices: 1; Exchanges: 1 fruit, 3 lean protein, 1 fat

Moist Bran Muffins

Servings: 12

Ingredients:

1 cup 1% low-fat milk

1 cup unprocessed wheat bran

2 teaspoons plus 1/4 cup canola oil, divided

1 cup whole wheat flour

1/4 cup packed light brown sugar

2 teaspoons baking powder

3/4 teaspoon ground cinnamon

1/4 teaspoon salt

2 large eggs

1/3 cup light or dark molasses (not blackstrap)

1 teaspoon vanilla extract

Directions:

1. Pour the milk into a medium saucepan and set over medium heat until hot but not boiling. Remove from the heat and stir in the bran. Cover and let stand 10 minutes.

2. Meanwhile, preheat the oven to 350°F. Brush a 12-cup muffin tin with 2 teaspoons of the oil or omit the oil and line the tin with paper muffin liners.

3. Combine the flour, sugar, baking powder, cinnamon, and salt in a large bowl and whisk to mix well. Combine the remaining 1/4 cup oil, the eggs, molasses, and vanilla in a medium bowl and whisk until smooth. Add the bran mixture to the oil mixture and stir to mix well. Add the bran mixture to the flour mixture and stir just until moistened. (The batter will be thin.)

4. Spoon the batter evenly into the muffin cups. Bake until a toothpick inserted into the centers of the muffins comes out clean, 20 to 22 minutes.

5. Cool the muffins in the pan on a wire rack for 5 minutes. Remove the muffins from the pan and place on the rack. Serve hot, warm, or at room temperature. The muffins can be stored in an airtight container at room temperature for up to 2 days or frozen for up to 3 months.

Nutrition Info:

23 g carb, 157 cal, 6 g fat, 1 g sat fat, 36 mg chol, 3 g fib, 4 g pro, 142 mg sod • Carb Choices: 1 1/2; Exchanges: 1 1/2 carb, 1 fat

Basic Boiled Beets

Servings: 4

Ingredients:

1-pound beets, well scrubbed (about 3 medium)

Directions:

1. Place the beets in a large saucepan and add water to cover. Bring to a boil over high heat. Reduce the heat to low, cover, and simmer until the beets are tender when pierced with a knife, about 1 hour.

2. Drain the beets in a colander. Cool slightly and use your hands to slip the skins off under cold running water.

Nutrition Info:

7 g carb, 33 cal, 0 g fat, 0 g sat fat, 0 mg chol, 2 g fib, 1 g pro, 59 mg sod • Carb Choices: 1/2; Exchanges: 1 vegetable

Lamb Chops with Blackberry-thyme Sauce

Servings: 4

Ingredients:

2 teaspoons extra virgin olive oil

1/3 cup minced shallot

1 garlic clove, minced

1/2 cup dry red wine

1/2 cup Beef Stock or low-sodium beef broth

2 tablespoons real maple syrup

1 (12-ounce) package unsweetened frozen blackberries, thawed

1 tablespoon cold water

1 teaspoon cornstarch

2 teaspoons chopped fresh thyme, divided

Pinch plus 1/2 teaspoon kosher salt, divided

Pinch plus 1/4 teaspoon freshly ground pepper, divided

8 (4-ounce) lamb rib chops, trimmed of all visible fat

Directions:

1. Heat a medium skillet over medium heat. Add the oil and tilt the pan to coat the bottom evenly. Add the shallot and cook, stirring often, until softened, about 3 minutes. Add the garlic and cook, stirring constantly, until fragrant, 30 seconds. Add the wine, stock, and maple syrup.

2. Reserve 1/2 cup of the blackberries and set aside. Add the remaining blackberries to the skillet. Bring to a boil and cook, crushing the berries with the back of a spoon, until the blackberry mixture is slightly thickened, 6 to 8 minutes.

3. Place a fine wire mesh strainer over a small saucepan and pour in the blackberry mixture.Press the mixture through the strainer, discarding the solids. Stir together the water and cornstarch in a small bowl until the cornstarch dissolves. Stir the cornstarch mixture into the sauce.

4. Set the saucepan over medium heat and cook, whisking constantly, until the sauce comes to a boil and thickens, 3 minutes. Stir in the reserved 1/2 cup blackberries, 1/2 teaspoon of the thyme, the pinch of salt, and the pinch of pepper and cook until the blackberries are heated through, 30 seconds.

5. Meanwhile, heat a large heavy-bottomed skillet over medium-high heat. Sprinkle the lamb chops with the remaining 1 1/2 teaspoons thyme, 1/2 teaspoon salt, and 1/4 teaspoon pepper. Cook the lamb 2 minutes on each side for medium rare, or to the desired degree of doneness. Divide the chops among 4 plates, drizzle evenly with the sauce, and serve at once.

Nutrition Info:

19 g carb, 286 cal, 10 g fat, 3 g sat fat, 94 mg chol, 0 g fib, 26 g pro, 262 mg sod •
Carb Choices: 1; Exchanges: 1/2 carb, 1/2 fruit, 3 lean protein, 1/2 fat

Broiled Beefsteak Tomatoes with Basil And Parmesan

Servings: 4

Ingredients:

Make this recipe only with peak-of-summer tomatoes and serve them as a centerpiece to a summer vegetable plate, or as a side dish with sautéed fish fillets or pan-seared steaks.

2 1/2 teaspoons extra virgin olive oil, divided

2 large beefsteak tomatoes, cut in half horizontally

1/2 teaspoon kosher salt

Pinch of freshly ground pepper

1 ounce freshly grated Parmesan (about 1/4 cup)

1 tablespoon chopped fresh basil

Directions:

1. Preheat the broiler. Brush a broiler pan with 1/2 teaspoon of the oil.

2. Brush the cut side of the tomatoes with the remaining 2 teaspoons oil and sprinkle with the salt and pepper. Place the tomatoes cut side up on the broiler pan and broil until the tomatoes begin to soften, about 6 minutes. Remove from the oven and sprinkle with the Parmesan. Broil until the cheese melts, 1 to 2 minutes longer.

3. Transfer the tomatoes to a serving platter and sprinkle with the basil. Serve hot, warm, or at room temperature.

Nutrition Info:

3 g carb, 35 cal, 2 g fat, 1 g sat fat, 0 mg chol, 1 g fib, 1 g pro, 144 mg sod • Carb Choices: 0; Exchanges: 1 veg, 1/2 fat

Mustard-molasses Grilled Chicken

Servings: 4

Ingredients:

1 tablespoon molasses

1 tablespoon whole grain mustard

4 (4-ounce) boneless skinless chicken breasts

1/2 teaspoon canola oil

1/2 teaspoon kosher salt

Directions:

1. Preheat the grill to medium-high heat.

2. Stir together the molasses and mustard in a shallow dish. Add the chicken and turn to coat. Let stand at room temperature for 15 minutes.

3. Brush the grill rack with the oil. Sprinkle the chicken with the salt, place on the grill, and grill, turning often, until the juices of the chicken run clear, 8 to 10 minutes. Divide the chicken among 4 plates and serve at once.

Nutrition Info:

4 g carb, 144 cal, 4 g fat, 1 g sat fat, 63 mg chol, 0 g fib, 23 g pro, 274 mg sod •
Carb Choices: 0; Exchanges: 3 lean protein

Salmon Baked In Tomato-fennel Sauce

Servings: 4

Ingredients:

2 teaspoons extra virgin olive oil

1 small onion, halved lengthwise and thinly sliced

1 small bulb fennel, tough outer leaves removed, cored and thinly sliced

1 garlic clove, minced

1/2 cup dry white wine

1/2 cup Chicken Stock or low-sodium chicken broth

1 large tomato, chopped

1/4 teaspoon kosher salt, divided

1/4 teaspoon freshly ground pepper, divided

4 (4-ounce) salmon fillets

1 teaspoon grated lemon zest

2 tablespoons chopped fresh Italian parsley

Directions:

1. Preheat the oven to 350°F.

2. Heat a large ovenproof skillet over medium-high heat. Add the oil and tilt the pan to coat the bottom evenly. Add the onion and fennel and cook, stirring often, until the vegetables are softened, 5 minutes. Add the garlic and cook, stirring constantly, until fragrant, 30 seconds. Add the wine and stock and bring to a boil. Stir in the tomato, 1/8 teaspoon of the salt, and 1/8 teaspoon of the pepper.

3. Sprinkle the salmon with the remaining 1/8 teaspoon salt, the remaining 1/8 teaspoon pepper, and the lemon zest. Place the salmon in a single layer on top of the vegetables. Cover with foil and bake until the fish is opaque in the center, 12 to 15 minutes.

4. Place the salmon in 4 shallow bowls. Stir the parsley into the vegetables remaining in the skillet and spoon evenly around the salmon. Serve at once.

Nutrition Info:

9 g carb, 268 cal, 11 g fat, 2 g sat fat, 72 mg chol, 3 g fib, 28 g pro, 179 mg sod • Carb Choices: 1/2; Exchanges: 1 veg, 4 lean protein, 1/2 fat

Multigrain Bread Stuffing with Mixed Mushrooms

Servings: 8

Ingredients:

1 cup water

1/2 ounce dried porcini mushrooms

6 cups 1/2-inch multigrain bread cubes

3 teaspoons extra virgin olive oil, divided

2 medium leeks, halved lengthwise and thinly sliced

6 ounces shiitake mushrooms, stemmed and thinly sliced

6 ounces cremini mushrooms, thinly sliced

1 tablespoon chopped fresh thyme or 1 1/2 teaspoons dried thyme

1/4 teaspoon kosher salt

1/8 teaspoons freshly ground pepper

1 cup Chicken Stock or low-sodium chicken broth

Directions:

1. Bring the water to a boil in a small saucepan over high heat. Remove from the heat, add the porcini mushrooms, cover, and let stand 30 minutes.

2. Meanwhile, preheat the oven to 350°F. Place the bread cubes in a single layer on a large rimmed baking sheet. Bake, stirring once, until the cubes are lightly toasted, 12 to 15 minutes. Set aside. Maintain the oven temperature.

3. Brush a 2-quart baking dish with 1 teaspoon of the oil.

4. Place a coffee filter in a fine wire mesh strainer and place over a bowl. Pour the mushroom mixture through the filter. Finely chop the mushrooms and reserve the mushroom soaking liquid.

5. Submerge the sliced leeks in a large bowl of water, lift them out, and drain in a colander. Repeat, using fresh water, until no grit remains in the bottom of the bowl. Drain the leeks well.

6. Heat a large nonstick skillet over medium heat. Add the remaining 2 teaspoons oil and tilt the pan to coat the bottom evenly. Add the shiitake and cremini mushrooms and the leeks and cook, stirring often, until the mushrooms are tender and most of the liquid has evaporated, 8 minutes. Stir in the thyme, salt, and pepper. Transfer the mixture to a large bowl and stir in the toasted bread cubes, soaked porcini mushrooms, reserved mushroom soaking liquid, and stock.

7. Spoon the stuffing into the prepared baking dish, cover with foil, and bake 20 minutes. Uncover and bake until the top of the stuffing is lightly browned, about 15 minutes longer. Serve at once.

Nutrition Info:

22 g carb, 119 cal, 3 g fat, 0 g sat fat, 1 mg chol, 7 g fib, 6 g pro, 164 mg sod • Carb Choices: 11/2; Exchanges: 1 starch, 1 veg, 1/2 fat

Steak Sandwiches with Tomato Jam

Servings: 4

Ingredients:

1 teaspoon grated lemon zest

2 tablespoons lemon juice

3 teaspoons extra virgin olive oil, divided

1 garlic clove, minced

1 (1-pound) flank steak, trimmed of all visible fat

1/2 teaspoon kosher salt

1/8 teaspoon freshly ground pepper

4 (1/2-inch) diagonally cut slices whole wheat Italian bread, toasted

2 cups loosely packed arugula

1/2 cup Tomato Jam

Directions:

1. Stir together the lemon zest, lemon juice, 1 teaspoon of the oil, and the garlic in a large shallow dish. Add the steak and turn to coat. Cover and refrigerate at least 6 hours or up to 12 hours.

2. Sprinkle the steak with the salt and pepper. Heat a large heavy-bottomed skillet over medium-high heat. Add the remaining 2 teaspoons oil and tilt the pan to coat the bottom evenly. Add the steak and cook, turning once, 4 minutes on each side for medium-rare, or to the desired degree of doneness.

3. Transfer the steak to a cutting board, cover loosely with foil, and let stand 5 minutes. Cut across the grain into thin slices.

4. Place the bread on each of 4 plates. Top each slice with 1/2 cup of the arugula. Top evenly with the steak. Top the steak evenly with the jam and serve at once.

Nutrition Info:

27 g carb, 337 cal, 13 g fat, 4 g sat fat, 43 mg chol, 4 g fib, 29 g pro, 348 mg sod • Carb Choices: 2; Exchanges: 1 starch, 1 carb, 3 medium-fat protein, 1/2 fat

Sharp Cheddar Macaroni And Cheese

Servings: 4

Ingredients:

1 teaspoon canola oil

6 ounces whole wheat macaroni or other short pasta (about 2 cups)

3⁄4 cup 1% low-fat milk

1 tablespoon unbleached all-purpose flour

4 ounces shredded extra-sharp Cheddar cheese (about 1 cup)

2 tablespoons reduced-fat cream cheese (about 1 ounce)

1⁄4 teaspoon kosher salt

1⁄4 teaspoon freshly ground pepper

2 tablespoons plain dry breadcrumbs

1 teaspoon unsalted butter, softened

2 tablespoons freshly grated Parmesan

Directions:

1. Preheat the oven to 350°F. Brush an 8-inch square baking dish with the oil.

2. Cook the pasta according to the package directions. Transfer to a bowl and keep warm.

3. Meanwhile, combine the milk and flour in a medium saucepan and whisk until smooth. Cook over medium heat, whisking constantly, until the mixture comes to a boil and thickens, about 5 minutes.

4. Remove from the heat. Add the Cheddar, cream cheese, salt, and pepper and whisk until smooth. Add the sauce to the macaroni and stir until well combined.

5. Transfer to the prepared baking dish. Combine the breadcrumbs and butter in a small bowl. Using your fingers, blend the butter evenly into the breadcrumbs. Stir in the Parmesan. Sprinkle the breadcrumb mixture over the pasta and bake until bubbly and heated through, about 25 minutes. Let stand 5 minutes before serving. Divide evenly among 4 plates and serve at once.

Nutrition Info:

38 g carb, 345 cal, 15 g fat, 9 g sat fat, 38 mg chol, 3 g fib, 16 g pro, 365 mg sod • Carb Choices: 21/2; Exchanges: 21/2 starch, 1 high-fat protein

Grilled Turkey Cutlets with Apple Salsa

Servings: 4

Ingredients:

Turkey:

1/4 cup unsweetened apple juice

2 tablespoons chopped fresh mint

2 garlic cloves, minced

1 1/2 teaspoons extra virgin olive oil, divided

1 teaspoon grated lime zest

4 (4-ounce) turkey breast cutlets

1/2 teaspoon kosher salt

Salsa:

2 medium Granny Smith apples, cored and chopped

2 tablespoons diced red onion

1 small jalapeño, seeded and minced

1 tablespoon chopped fresh mint

1 tablespoon lime juice

1 teaspoon extra virgin olive oil

1/8 teaspoon kosher salt

Directions:

1. To make the turkey, combine the apple juice, mint, garlic, 1 teaspoon of the oil, and the lime zest in a large resealable plastic bag. Add the turkey, turn to coat, and refrigerate 2 to 4 hours.

2. Preheat the grill to medium-high heat.

3. Remove the turkey from the marinade and discard the marinade. Pat the turkey dry with paper towels and sprinkle with the salt.

4. Brush the grill rack with the remaining 1/2 teaspoon oil. Place the turkey on the grill and grill, turning often, until no longer pink, 8 to 10 minutes.

5. Meanwhile, to make the salsa, combine all the ingredients in a medium bowl and stir to combine. Divide the turkey among 4 plates and serve with the salsa.

Nutrition Info:

13 g carb, 153 cal, 2 g fat, 0 g sat fat, 34 mg chol, 2 g fib, 21 g pro, 252 mg sod • Carb Choices: 1; Exchanges: 1 fruit, 3 lean protein

Creamy Vegetable Chowder

Servings: 4

Ingredients:

2 teaspoons extra virgin olive oil

1 medium onion, chopped

1 garlic clove, minced

2 cups Vegetable Stock or low-sodium vegetable broth

12 ounces turnips, peeled and chopped

2 carrots, peeled and chopped

1 stalk celery, chopped

1/8 teaspoon dried thyme

1/2 teaspoon kosher salt

1/8 teaspoon freshly ground pepper

1 cup 1% low-fat milk

1 tablespoon unbleached all-purpose flour

2 tablespoons chopped fresh Italian parsley

Directions:

1. Heat a large pot over medium heat. Add the oil and tilt the pan to coat the bottom evenly. Add the onion and cook, stirring often, until softened, 5 minutes. Add the garlic and cook, stirring constantly, until fragrant, 30 seconds. Add the stock, turnips, carrots, celery, thyme, salt, and pepper and bring to a boil over high heat. Cover, reduce the heat to low, and simmer until the vegetables are tender, 20 minutes.

2. Whisk together the milk and flour in a small bowl. Add to the soup and return to a simmer. Cook, stirring often, just until slightly thickened, about 3 minutes. Remove from the heat and stir in the parsley. Ladle into 4 bowls and serve at once. The soup can be refrigerated, covered, for up to 4 days.

Nutrition Info:

14 g carb, 98 cal, 3 g fat, 1 g sat fat, 2 mg chol, 3 g fib, 4 g pro, 334 mg sod • Carb Choices: 1; Exchanges: 1/2 carb, 1 veg, 1/2 fat

Chicken And Vegetable Wraps with Sun-dried Tomato-basil Spread

Servings: 4

Ingredients:

1/4 cup dry-packed sun-dried tomatoes, minced

1/4 cup water

4 ounces reduced-fat cream cheese, softened

1/4 teaspoon kosher salt, divided

1/4 teaspoon freshly ground pepper, divided

2 tablespoons chopped fresh basil

2 teaspoons extra virgin olive oil

3 (4-ounce) boneless skinless chicken breasts

4 (8-inch) whole wheat flour tortillas

8 leaves Bibb lettuce

1/2 hothouse (English) cucumber, very thinly sliced

Directions:

1. Combine the tomatoes and water in a small saucepan. Set over medium heat and bring to a boil over high heat. Remove from the heat, cover, and let stand 15 minutes. Drain the tomatoes.

2. Combine the tomatoes, cream cheese, 1/8 teaspoon of the salt, and 1/8 teaspoon of the pepper in a small bowl and stir until smooth. Stir in the basil.

3. Meanwhile, sprinkle the chicken with the remaining 1/8 teaspoon salt and remaining 1/8 teaspoon pepper. Heat a large nonstick skillet over medium- high heat. Add the oil and tilt the pan to coat the bottom evenly.

4. Add the chicken and cook until the juices run clear, 4 minutes on each side. Cut into thin slices.

5. Spread each tortilla with a generous tablespoon of cream cheese mixture. Top with the lettuce leaves, cucumber slices, and chicken. Roll up and cut each roll in half.

Nutrition Info:

28 g carb, 343 cal, 14 g fat, 6 g sat fat, 63 mg chol, 6 g fib, 26 g pro, 727 mg sod •
Carb Choices: 1 1/2; Exchanges: 1 1/2 starch, 2 lean protein, 2 fat

Apple-spice Cake

Servings: 16

Ingredients:

2 teaspoons plus 1⁄3 cup canola oil, divided

1 1⁄4 cups unbleached all-purpose flour plus flour for dusting pan

3⁄4 cup whole wheat flour

2 teaspoons baking powder

1 teaspoon baking soda

1 teaspoon ground cinnamon

1⁄2 teaspoon ground allspice

1⁄4 teaspoon salt

1⁄2 cup granulated sugar

1⁄2 cup packed light brown sugar

1⁄2 cup plain low-fat yogurt

2 large eggs

2 large apples, peeled, cored, and coarsely shredded (about 1 1⁄4 cups)

Directions:

1. Preheat the oven to 350°F. Brush a 10- or 12-cup Bundt pan with 2 teaspoons of the oil. Dust the pan lightly with all-purpose flour, shaking the pan to remove the excess.

2. Combine the 1 1/4 cups all-purpose flour, whole wheat flour, baking powder, baking soda, cinnamon, allspice, and salt in a large bowl and whisk to mix well.

3. Combine the granulated sugar, brown sugar, the remaining 1/3 cup oil, the yogurt, and eggs in a medium bowl and whisk until smooth. Add the sugar mixture to the flour mixture and stir just until the batter is moist. Stir in the apples.

4. Spoon the batter into the prepared pan and bake until a wooden toothpick inserted in the center of the cake comes out clean, 40 to 45 minutes. Cool the cake in the pan on a wire rack for 10 minutes. Remove from the pan and cool completely on a wire rack before slicing. The cake can be covered in an airtight container and stored at room temperature for up to 3 days.

Nutrition Info:

27 g carb, 172 cal, 6 g fat, 1 g sat fat, 27 mg chol, 1 g fib, 3 g pro, 182 mg sod • Carb Choices: 2; Exchanges: 2 carb, 1 fat

Greek Steak Sandwiches

Servings: 4

Ingredients:

1 (1-pound) flank steak, trimmed of all visible fat

1/4 teaspoon kosher salt

1/8 teaspoon freshly ground pepper

2 teaspoons canola oil

1/2 cup plain low-fat yogurt

2 teaspoons grated lemon zest

4 (1/2-inch) diagonally cut slices whole wheat Italian bread, toasted

2 cups thinly sliced romaine lettuce

2 plum tomatoes, sliced

1/2 hothouse (English) cucumber, thinly sliced

4 pepperoncini peppers, drained and thinly sliced

1 ounce finely crumbled feta cheese (about 1/4 cup)

Directions:

1. Sprinkle the steak with the salt and pepper. Heat a large heavy-bottomed skillet over medium-high heat. Add the oil and tilt the pan to coat the bottom evenly. Add the steak and cook, turning once, 4 minutes on each side for medium-rare, or to the desired degree of doneness.

2. Transfer the steak to a cutting board, cover loosely with foil, and let stand 5 minutes. Cut across the grain into thin slices.

3. Meanwhile, stir together the yogurt and lemon zest in a small bowl.

4. Place the bread on each of 4 plates. Top each slice evenly with the lettuce, tomatoes, cucumber, and pepperoncini. Top evenly with the steak, drizzle with the yogurt mixture, and sprinkle with the feta. Serve at once.

Nutrition Info:

13 g carb, 281 cal, 13 g fat, 5 g sat fat, 57 mg chol, 2 g fib, 29 g pro, 398 mg sod • Carb Choices: 1; Exchanges: 1 starch, 3 lean protein, 1 fat

Breakfast Barley with Honey And Walnuts

Servings: 4

Ingredients:

2/3 cup pearl barley

2 cups water

2 tablespoons currants

Pinch of kosher salt

1 tablespoon honey

2 tablespoons walnuts, toasted and chopped

Directions:

1. Place the barley in a medium saucepan and set over medium heat. Toast, shaking the pan often, until the barley is lightly browned and fragrant, 5 minutes.

2. Add the water, currants, and salt and bring to a boil over high heat. Reduce the heat to low, cover, and simmer until the barley is tender, 20 to 25 minutes. Stir in the honey.

3. Spoon the barley into 4 bowls and sprinkle evenly with the walnuts. Serve at once.

Nutrition Info:

34 g carb, 170 cal, 3 g fat, 0 g sat fat, 0 mg chol, 6 g fib, 4 g pro, 21 mg sod • Carb Choices: 2; Exchanges: 2 starch, 1/2 fat

Lemon-spice Roasted Turkey

Servings: 12

Ingredients:

Turkey

2 garlic cloves, minced

2 tablespoons grated lemon zest

2 teaspoons ground cumin

2 teaspoons kosher salt

1 teaspoon ground coriander

1/2 teaspoon freshly ground pepper

1 (12-pound) whole turkey

2 large lemons, quartered

1/2 teaspoon canola oil

Gravy

3 cups Chicken Stock or low-sodium chicken broth

1/4 cup unbleached all-purpose flour

3 tablespoons chopped fresh Italian parsley

1 teaspoon grated lemon zest

1/2 teaspoon kosher salt

1/4 teaspoon freshly ground pepper

Directions:

1. To make the turkey, preheat the oven to 325°F.

2. Combine the garlic, lemon zest, cumin, salt, coriander, and pepper in a small bowl. Remove and discard the neck and giblets from the cavity of the turkey. Loosen the skin from the breast and drumsticks by inserting your fingers and gently separating the skin from the meat. Rub the garlic mixture over the breast and drumsticks underneath the skin.

3. Place the lemons inside the cavity. Tuck the wing tips underneath the turkey and tie the legs together with kitchen string.

4. Brush a wire roasting rack with the oil. Place the turkey on the rack in a large roasting pan. Cover the turkey breast with foil and bake 1 1/2 hours. Remove the foil and bake until a thermometer inserted into a thigh registers 165°F, 1 hour to 1 hour 15 minutes. Transfer to a serving platter and cover loosely with foil while preparing the gravy. Discard the lemons.

5. To make the gravy, remove the rack from the roasting pan. Pour the pan drippings into a fat separator or a glass measuring cup. Pour off and discard the fat. Add enough of the stock to make 3 1/4 cups. Pour the stock mixture into the roasting pan. Add the flour and whisk until smooth. Set the roasting pan over two burners and cook over medium-high heat, whisking constantly, until the gravy comes to a boil and thickens, about 8 minutes. Stir in the parsley, lemon zest, salt, and pepper. Carve the turkey and serve with the gravy. Remove the skin from the turkey before eating.

Nutrition Info:

1 g carb, 180 cal, 3 g fat, 1 g sat fat, 112 mg chol, 0 g fib, 34 g pro, 211 mg sod • Carb Choices: 0; Exchanges: 5 lean protein

Watermelon Agua Fresca

Servings: 4

Ingredients:

4 cups 3⁄4-inch cubes seedless watermelon

1 cup cold water

1 1⁄2 tablespoons lime juice

Directions:

1. Combine all the ingredients in a blender in batches and process until smooth. Transfer to a pitcher. Serve over ice.

Nutrition Info:

14 g carb, 41 cal, 0 g fat, 0 g sat fat, 0 mg chol, 1 g fib, 1 g pro, 5 mg sod • Carb Choices: 1; Exchanges: 1 fruit

Pasta, Vegetable, And Goat Cheese Gratin

Servings: 6

Ingredients:

3 teaspoons extra virgin olive oil, divided

8 ounces whole wheat penne or other short pasta (about 2 2/3 cups)

1 medium eggplant, peeled and cut into 1/2-inch cubes

1 medium zucchini, quartered lengthwise and sliced

1 medium onion, halved lengthwise and thinly sliced

2 garlic cloves, minced

1 large tomato, chopped

1/4 cup Kalamata olives, pitted and quartered

1/2 teaspoon dried thyme

1/2 teaspoon kosher salt

1/8 teaspoon freshly ground pepper

4 ounces crumbled goat cheese (about 1 cup)

2 tablespoons freshly grated Parmesan

Directions:

1. Preheat the oven to 350°F. Brush a 13 x 9-inch baking dish with 1 teaspoon of the oil.

2. Cook the pasta according to the package directions. Transfer to a large bowl.

3. Meanwhile, heat a large nonstick skillet over medium-high heat. Add the remaining 2 teaspoons oil and tilt the pan to coat the bottom evenly. Add the eggplant, zucchini, and onion and cook, stirring often, until the vegetables are crisp-tender, 8 minutes. Add the garlic and cook, stirring constantly, until fragrant, 30 seconds.

4. Add the vegetable mixture, tomato, olives, thyme, salt, and pepper to the pasta and toss to combine. Add the goat cheese and toss to combine.

5. Transfer to the prepared baking dish. Sprinkle with the Parmesan and bake until the cheese melts and the top is lightly browned, 20 to 25 minutes. Spoon the gratin evenly onto 6 plates and serve at once.

Nutrition Info:

32 g carb, 273 cal, 11 g fat, 5 g sat fat, 16 mg chol, 7 g fib, 12 g pro, 304 mg sod • Carb Choices: 2; Exchanges: 1 1/2 starch, 1 veg, 1 medium-fat protein, 1/2 fat

Romano–black Pepper Biscotti

Servings: 24

Ingredients:

1 1/2 cups white whole wheat flour or unbleached all-purpose flour

1 ounce freshly grated Pecorino Romano (about 1/4 cup)

1 teaspoon baking powder

1/2 teaspoon salt

1/4 teaspoon freshly ground pepper

1/4 cup extra virgin olive oil

1/4 cup 1% low-fat milk

1 large egg

1 garlic clove, crushed through a press

Directions:

1. Preheat the oven to 350°F. Line a large baking sheet with parchment paper.

2. Combine the flour, Pecorino Romano, baking powder, salt, and pepper in a large bowl and whisk to mix well. Combine the oil, milk, egg, and garlic in a medium bowl and whisk until smooth.

3. Add the oil mixture to the flour mixture and stir just until the dough is moistened and holds together. Place the dough on the prepared baking sheet, press into a 12-inch log, and press on the log to flatten it slightly.

4. Bake until the top is lightly browned, 25 to 30 minutes. Remove from the baking sheet and transfer to a wire rack. Let cool until just slightly warm, about 20 minutes.

5. Reduce the oven temperature to 325°F.

6. Cut the log diagonally into 24 (1/2-inch) slices using a serrated knife. Place on a parchment-lined baking sheet and bake 20 minutes. Turn the biscotti and bake until lightly browned, 10 to 15 minutes longer. Remove from the baking sheet and transfer to a wire rack to cool completely. The biscotti can be stored in an airtight container at room temperature for up to 3 days.

Nutrition Info:

12 g carb, 118 cal, 6 g fat, 1 g sat fat, 21 mg chol, 2 g fib, 4 g pro, 182 mg sod • Carb Choices: 1; Exchanges: 1 starch, 1 fat

Alphabetical Index

L

M

O

P

R

S

T

W

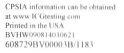
CPSIA information can be obtained
at www.ICGtesting.com
Printed in the USA
BVHW090814030621
608729BV00003B/1183